Walking in the World

WALKING IN
THE WORLD

and an Oxygen Jar

A collection of poems by Laraine Kentridge Lasdon

larainelasdon@gmail.com

Copyright © 2025 Laraine Kentridge Lasdon
Printed in the United States of America
First Edition

ISBN 979-8-218-67297-3

First Printing, 2025

For my late husband Leon and my daughter
Claire always there in spirit and space

Contents

Walking in the World

The Oxygen Jar

I thought I was a complex being,
seeing my body in the mirror,
watching blood dribble into vials,
rich and red as a Queen's cape.
A needle is pricking into a vein
revealing an interior landscape
of metabolic processes balanced
to generate energy and efficiency,
hardly radical enough to notice
the simple, capricious breath.

Breath is subtle
Subject to muddle and turbulence
of emotions that course through blood,
pumping oxygen like the ancestral
gill of the fish. Heka, Egyptian
god of magic and medicine,
used breath as a power sustaining life
and the universe. Always present,
even as I feel it's absence.

 I feel your breath leaving you,
my hands cradling your face,
my lips close to yours,
you lie still and calm in death.
My breath seems to have stopped.
A shocking mysterious force
generates a rush of air, involuntary,
an alchemy of complexity.

Unlike the insect in the
oxygen jar who dies when deprived
of air, I am the mint leaf
in the oxygen jar, growing, thriving,
pushing against the closed black lid.
Grief wants to bury me
but breath can hibernate,
reclaim, expel and inhale!
Life towards life.

Walking in the World

The way you walked in the world
said everything about you.
Broad strides, bright eyes,
noticing with generosity
everything around you.
Moving through rough times
with quiet understanding and patience.
Enjoying friendships and conversation
with attention and acceptance.

All seasons wrapped around you
like silks and brocades.
You walked through the cultures of India,
Japan, Europe and your adopted
hometowns of Cleveland and Austin
sharing wisdom, innovation
with colleagues and scholars,
unselfishly, patiently, always the professor.

The way you walked through the world
seemed to be a pilgrimage,
quiet and steady,
the way you gave to the world,
this is your legacy.

I Don't Know

To spring from the green lawn,
knees bent, crouched for the leap,
the stretch of my body is exhilarating!
I relish my outward show of strength.
Laughing, I land on the grass, fooling
myself, the world, the universe.

"Can I help you find your true self"?
"Who is asking"?
Where is this disembodied voice
coming from? I am no longer jovial,
mouth turned down in a sulk.
A child found out; I spilled the milk.

I hardly remember happiness.
Scratchy, ephemeral moments,
sun flash, the heat of possibilities,
then gone. Sadness seems to last forever,
a Dali landscape. Distorted perceptions.
Days abnormally long.

"Is this the life you are living"
said the voice, persistent, not revealing
the meaning, adding that:
Sadly, I have limited time
for fear, for anger, complaint.
The calendar, the clocks
are tick tock dictators.
But if I get the answer right
before I touch the sun,
or hold close the restful night,
when time will abandon the cold,
incessant measurement
of the scythe of Cronos,
heart heat will warm new growth.

So, I give the best answer I can,
in an honest, humble tone,
not knowing what was right or wrong.
The words come out steady and slow,
I said, to the voice, I said to myself:
the answer is: "I don't know"

The Red Candle

I watched her light
a fine red candle,
it's flame wavering
as she placed her hands
in prayer above the small blaze.

Crimson wax drips,
sizzles on cold silver,
sealing the memory
of her gentle husband
this Sabbath night,
reflecting the glow
of the ruby ring, her birthstone,
his last gift, their last summer.

She began murmuring words
of gratitude for life, for breath,
birth and death, her sing song
voice creating a sacred space,
trying to believe that time would heal.

The flame of the candle
is lustrous, burning
now red, green, silver,
white hot, a faint hiss
counterpoint to her hushed
invocations, its glow a kiss
on her gentle lips.

Musings

Dark brooding
or bright hope
emotions' decibels
should be beautiful
a choir in your head
transmitting endless songs
virtual melodies
to remind you
what you can do
your power
in the world
shared as early
as 5am as the sun appears
and you turn on the radio
to fill the silence.

Musings continued:

I feel no tenderness for my younger self
beneath the rumblings of hurts,
parental discontent
with my lack of prettiness
my existence ambushed
their lives. No way out.

Musings continued:

Floating in the liminal phase
betwixt and between
rites of separation
loss of love
I visit the mind's mortuary
a sort of holding place
for dead hopes and dreams
waiting for the ending ceremony
so re-birth can begin
but, of course, it doesn't.

The eye opens
The heart beats
Defeated by death
A new drama begins

"....give sorrow words"

Let grief shine on the widow,
pierce the darkness of the word.
I add the letter "n" and create window,
which welcomes light and darkness
in equal measure, opens and closes
in all weathers. But lingering linguistics
confines and defines a cut out of a heart
and mind.

Let grief shine as fullness on the widow
'Widowe" to be empty.

Let grief shine as the wealth of life
"Vidh" to be destitute

Let grief shine as the precursor to joy
"Viduus" to be bereft

Longing

As old as creation
as ancient as the gods
as sensuous as the blue lotus
of Egypt, as delicate as the
perfumes of Persia,
as sonorous as the bells
of a thousand churches,
this is the deep emotion
we call longing.

A longing for peace.
A longing for freedom.
A yearning for power,
A desire for love
are all catastrophic
to the human soul
which cannot contain
the fluidity of longing – it flows through us,
it seeks Truth in us.
Longing is mercurial – ever changing.
From joy, to pain, desire to anguish.

I found longing in an abandoned
part of my heart and when the hurt
of loss touched me it came alive,
a strange creature coiled and uncoiled
in the deepest crevasses of my being.
It cannot die – it is not matter,
it does not matter what I want. I must
seek to befriend it, accept it, invite it in,
connect with it in all it's guises.
Until the sweet longing of hope
lightens the darkness.

The Intruder

My protector was Talos,
created by the gods,
wearing metallic armor
to ward off intruders,
then summoned by me
to fend off intrusions of hurt
and the uncertainty of the future.

The shadow of the intruder
shape-shifts into an aloneness,
a stranger, yet known,
yes, not entirely unknown,
beckoning me to follow
a loss line, perceived as a marked path,
withered signposts hinting at dead ends,
Cul de sacs, and an option to keep walking
straight through time itself.

The lost days are long, elastic.
Nocturnal apparitions appear,
evaporate. Devastation, deaths
and disasters clamor for attention.
What is a dream? What is not?

So I begin with the big things,
the love of a daughter, family
connections and gathering,
each loved one sharing the darkest void,
sheltering me from the worst of this war.

I also find most overlooked moments.
The small things: reading a book to the end,
a glass of wine, a phone call from a friend,
a focus on the lives of others becomes the lifeline,
blurring the loss line.

The intruder is both my sorrow
and the intruder is my hope,
offering a way to reach, to teach me
how the big things and the small things

merge, days focus, nights restful,
brackets of sun and moon defined.

No need for Talos to hurl storms of tears
to crush the enemy. My shapeshifting
intruder shines a light on clarity,
the *present* is where to begin again.
A reminder that tragedy drifts further away
from year to year. We live, but never forget.

The Last Second

It turns out life is both beautiful
and menacing. Misremembered memories
fill space between days, months and years,
otherwise filled with youthful noisy courage,
a promenade of lovers, until I no longer
want to be the outsider. Looking
and finding the partner I can understand
as deeply as day and night,
who I love and fight with,
build and destroy,
hate and love again, for decades,
assembling all the while, the structure of a life
that is more improvised than planned.

Love, beautiful in its imperfections,
blinded me to the challenge of death,
a hellish certainty for which I had no fix.
Nauseous, fearful, alone, I face
a future ghastly in it's perfection.

I wonder if there is even one second left
for hope, for human connection,
for faith. Or a realization that there will
never again be a "we" but only an "I'
Or is this a simple end of life silence.

Metamorphosis Re-visited

It's a daunting feeling
facing a recurring dream
walking along a path
haunted by the sound
of my percussive sobbing
the swish of dry brush
under my feet a heavy tread
the rhythm of fear and need

I want to be precise
about the insect dream
that they are black
their shiny carapace cracks
under my shoe as I stamp
on them and watch the blood
dark and sticky pool on the floor

The nightmare of crushed insects
threaten but, always, magically
metamorphize into butterflies
unfolding wings large and strong
purple, pink, indigo, carmine.
Cathedrals of color.

The dream repeats, recurs.
I stamp out the killer insects
and every time a butterfly emerges
flying over the transitional divide
between fear and strength
the dream fades away
a soft sunrise glow
itself a chrysalis, begins a new day.

Lace Song

The explosion
        of my
             heart
when you died
stopped birds
        in mid-air
a forest of willow trees
        turned as black as widows' weeds
and clouds
        twisted into tight, thin threads

I lay
        very still
until my breath touched
        the wingtip of a lark
it's song like a bobbin
        weaving melody
creating lace from ash
        trees found their bright green
and my eyes
        noticed
the silver lining of the soft clouds

Thought Blossoms

My thoughts are of loss, grief,
a fiefdom of dark, resonant cello chords
only I can hear.
But in the naked red of sunset,
I float into a chamber of silent
conversations, inaudible
acoustic sounds, awkward echoes,
transmissions for solo travelers,
following a sorrow map,
a cul de sac, unchangeable.

Invisible markers of an unknown future.

Phases of the moon, predictable,
observable, waning and waxing,
dazzling in moonlit fullness,
swelling, illuminated and repeating.

Visible markers of futures to come.

There are thoughts like spring blossoms.
Puffs of pinks
sprouting from bare bark.

Visible markers of futures to come.

Elpis, a goddess once trapped,
holds out her perfumed bouquet,
a symbol of her choice to stay.
Her freedom from Pandora's box,
her flowers, offer me a choice

to rejoin the visible, to choose hope.

Life Happens Every Day

Life happens every day
watch an egg being fried
really watch an egg being fried
its golden yolk and ragged edge of white
a simmering volcano in a crater of butter
which I slide off the pan into the trash

Life happens every day
I tell myself this while planting
rosemary and sage because they don't die
sweeping dried leaves off the porch
trying to make room to believe
that the swish of the straw broom
can make up for the empty space that was you

Life happens every day
plastic bags, newspapers
just crumpled creatures
old milk cartons and readymade words
tossed to the side
the leftovers hiding
in the green recycling bag
will never feed my hungry heart

Life happens every day
a potter's world of coiled clay
tokens, talismans, isolation guardians
not easily broken and discarded

Life happens every day
as I die inside

From Loss to Life

Walk through bleak cedar brush
They say "through the valley of the shadow of death"
From winter to spring
Don't speak of a summer to come

Observe injuries so severe
Wrinkle and knot in the fabric of heart
Start along a slim path
Not a soul in sight, alone
On your own

Reach the final pit
Of emotional distress
Dark and brooding
Move around it
Following breath
Away from death

The cedar is perfumed
There are people to be seen
How can you help them
When stones are bones
You are part of Kehila, community
Be here, be here. Hineini.

The Art of Being Left Behind

2025 One year later

Looking back: part one

I started journaling my journey
the day after I sat at the hospice bed,
tracked his rasping breaths,
spaces between breaths,
until the space became death,
and he doesn't whisper "I love you" and "be happy"
and "I don't blame you"

It could have been any day, that first day.
A murder of widows, widowers, keening on day one,
filled with a strange pain, a brew of unease,
brooding, a contrast of frantic movement,
discarding clothes, shoes, belts and ties.
The bathrobe on the hook, the half-used soap
sticky in the now dry shower.
Yet I don't erase
the impression of his head
on the pillowcase.

Dread and panic mixed with cold control of files,
forms, funds. Everything he did day after day,
filing documents, pages of documents,
in heavy green cabinets.
Now I deal with attorneys, CPA's, universities, and the IRS.

We purchased this ground when it seemed ridiculous,
Even frivolous, but we did it "for the future"
smiling, should we pay the bill or not?
He had cancer and did not seem ill, but we bought the plot.

The funeral: a year ago

At the cemetery friends and family gather to mourn.
Solemn groups attended the funeral to remember him,
to show their respect. For the living and the dead.
To huddle around the small marker
fluttering in the winter wind.
To watch as ashes in a pink alabaster urn
carved Himalayan salt like salt of the earth
will become the earth
in its space of turned soil,
cold and damp on this February day.

They came for tea to keep me and each other
company for a congenial hour
while I drifted around the room, unmoored.
Then wrapped in coats and scarves
A gaggle of friendly scarecrows
they took their leave
these good friends and family.

The first night the questions come.
Did I do enough?
Did I love enough?
I re-live the last months.
I think of his withdrawing, fatigue,
becoming very quiet – quieter than usual.
"It's age' we said lightly. But the images
of him sleeping are stark.
Distended belly, puffy breaths, extended over
such a brief time when our visitor,
Death, was with us, but at a respectful distance.
I was worried, anxious, angry, but could not
remove it's presence or even recognize
it at first. Then I knew.

I railed against the facts, fought with doctors,
stroked my beloved's swollen stomach,
begged for new pills, infusions or trials
but to no avail. And so the day arrived
though I strived to fend it off

The last hour:

In the evening, the final hour,
I held his hand
kissed his dear head
not a peaceful sleep
but the end.
A permanent, forever end.

The Deep Growl of Grief

She was curious about the deep growl of grief
rumbling through her as if she had swallowed
the cello solo from a Shostakovich Largo movement
evoking concentration camps in 1944.
The miasma of the music stains her body
the moss green of a dying tree.
She is anchored to the ground,
unable to flee, as if she murdered her beloved
and cannot atone for he is gone and only
the deepest bass notes of a sacred oratorio
fall at her feet as autumn leaves
settling on gnarled burls,
nourishing dry roots
with the last sap of summer.

She thought she was guilty of envy
of beautiful Aphrodite,
her notorious list of bewitched lovers,
of her body cool with sea foam.
But her love was a mortal,
to love and adore,
a man she was fated to lose.

Now a widow, black-wrapped
in diaphanous drapes,
she did not aspire to emulate
Aphrodite. She wept, accepted
the eternal void but could not give
up hope that one night, standing in her
bed of leaves, she would look up,
see the sparkle of a star or at the
end of the darkest night
see the reb orb of a sun,
feel the fire of loss burn hot and fierce
until merciful rains fall, leaves curl,
and the majesty of life will unfurl
as the last notes of the cello
drift to a close.

www.ingramcontent.com/pod-product-compliance
Lightning Source LLC
Chambersburg PA
CBHW061723120626
46550CB00003B/1338